THE ZBÄD

THE ZBÄD

Darkness Forever

(The completion of 66 Sphinxes von Rhode Island.)

Archalien Kessle

Print information available on the last page.

Rev. date: 12/09/2016

To order additional copies of this book, contact:
Xlibris
1-888-795-4274
www.Xlibris.com
Orders@Xlibris.com
748067

"Ying is pair; in light of the incomparable yang." -Plutarch

Darkness Forever:

On Top of the sky,....
Ra the Sun God,
And Calendar his Moon-Goddess
Gave birth to two sons.
Kawa-Kawa and Tezcatlipoca.
Which means the Sole of a Jaguar.
A million stars were wrought before them;
And a million stars were wrought afterwards.
Cast down to the earth to sully mates!
They were given the spirit of wolves and
tongues of snakes!
But then one day when the boys were fishing...
They were swallowed by a whale.
A giant whale by the name of Isotropous.
When the older people heard about it,..
Everyone figured them to be destroyed&....
Never to be seen again.
In Virgo:
Before the execution of the Agorean altruist
P.J.,
and his burrow of 700 concubine... +
¿ men were bold,... (Turn water into wine)_o.p.
The women were ''gregarious,''
And (v) chaining path(z) of the Agorean sun was
normal & trust worthy.
But after.. ''The Event,''
The execution of P.J. and his 700 s
πlegal¿
concubines;..
The natuπal perfection of Agora was
consequently
trampled by the worst drought any of us had
eveπ seen.
After Obi had decided to behead P.J. on top of
the
Headless Triangle,...
Cutting off his head,..Δ
Then afterwards having 10 Bears remove his
heart,...

1

Then taking it from him,..
And violently waving it around
at all of the remaining Agorean woman;...
(And giving them a speech for everyone to see)
"Finally I can see why!!!"
''Finally I can see why it is P.J. the pathetic-
witch_bearer
who is intimate with every woman of Agora!'''
Finally I can see! He said teasing them
"Finally I can see why for the time being!"
He said before launching his heart off the top of
the Headless Triangle.
But afterwards,..
After Obi and I celebrated with some of the
moπe cold-blooded natives,..
Celebrated because the unsymmetrical reign of
P.J. the Agorean altruist, and
the banishing of t¶is boonie hordom was finally
over,...
......
''The impurity of the sacrifice sunk into everyone."
Knell;
By decapitating P.J.
and blaspheming his soul on top of the
Headless Triangle;..
The disciplined Sol-Adders had completely
defiled nobility;
''Celebrated insanity;''..
And also forgetting to remember their own
symbolism...
Our Flag,..
The African Bull....
(the beast that insinuates polygamy....) €
"Then so the following day,..."
Because of the polar whiff moπally,/
"blatant hypocrisy;..."
Our delightful Sol-Adder streams,
flowing rivers,
& hammocked creeks turned red with blood,
And we were all trampled by the worst drought
any of us had ever seen,..

Trampled because of the tradition of evil on top
of the Headless Triangle.
"Don't act so jaded Red Jay."
said Obi tossing him a bottled water;
And coming over to look out the window with
me.
"Are you coming back to "The Event" next
year Red Jay?"
He said cracking a smile
''I've got 300 more prisoners who have
posthumous[ly given themselves
to P.J.'s [l] pitiful-nympho-regime.''
''I'm not so sure I'll be going to that one Obi.''
(I said looking angrily at him and his
crude smirk..)
O yea Orenstein???
Why,
''Because the Obi always has to take cosmic
ownership over all Agora?''
''All Agora by myself because my brother Red
Jay refuses to be an extravagant lion?''
A supported Lion who never looks away from an
execution??.....
I never did, forsooth! (Obi said glaring at me)
''Life and death are synonymous Orenstein;...''
..
Next time, I'd advise you not to shake hands if
you aren't prepared to weather the storm...
''To weather tha spiritual burden until it bears
fruit!"
"Obi, all you've ever cared about is your own
demonic ambition;" "..Individually emancipated by
your own own cleverness;
while the rest of the world dies trying to compete
inside your l galactic maize or something."
Maybe next time instead of gambling with
peoples lives, maybe it's time to stop avoiding
your own rooster.
"Stand behind me Satan!!" Obi shouted
"Exactly Obi."
Make no mistake about it Red Jay!

"Forsooth!"
"Shaking hands with you is like shaking hands
with (a) l Agorean woman!"
As soon as things get a little testy & intimidating
for you;..
All you do is bitch and moan, bitch and moan
like a fucken dick head...
"Acting like there's no such thing as a social
science
when it comes to remaining the rightful King
of all Agora!"
"Please Obi!"
'I've never seen such an unsympathetic
narcissist!
(Obi laughed)
Red Jay, just remind me never to choose virtue
over futile propriety
next time life throws another ironic disease at
everyone."
**Us and those who can't live without the Mooπ's
h.o.a.π.
constitution of invariable autocracy."
Virtue!!!??? Red Jay stomped
"Agora is our home Obi."

"So what Red Jay?"
I beg your pardon???

What bitch? Instead of eradicating a currency of
estuary treason I nipped
the whole thing in the butt? Δ
...
Nipped the whole P.J thing in the butt like a
¿ pro??
Behold,
"No one wants to hear about your insecurity
problems Red Jay."
Agora iz expansive.
"So you literally aren't concerned about that
drought out there?"
"And the 700 she-deaths on top of the Headless

Triangle is just martial taboo?"
Onyx said for us not to worry about it Red Jay;...

...

"He said it's lame to even acknowledge the loss
of a couple
¿ hos when ultimately we're trying
to lock down viable goddesses for the afterlife
who can actfully handle th[e indigenous/
Agorean life-style.
''Behold!''...
(e said lowering the si_ fiddle..)
"I know we've taken a hit because of The Event
Red Jay." he whispered
"Onyx didn't say that Obi."
"And who knows if we'll even need women in the
afterlife."
Satan Red Ja''!!!.... grrrrr
(Obi stopped to think for a moment,..)
(Sensing his brother was already
a l bit fragile)
...You know what I mean now don't you
bud?????
"Come on now Red Jay."
Im talkin 'all time status!'
"Big girls and big boys !"
"Obi, its just
that directing this ridiculous offering to Monism
of ours
got a little out of hand over in Riverdale and I..."
"Shhhhhhhh"
said Obi trying to temper me with his 'can't trick'
Adder-Lord
empathy. Δ
''All I wanted was to feel unimpeded by ass...''
''Impeded by all P.J.'s no-moccasin parties.'' ''I
know
bud,''
''we are now.''
And now that everyone's getting tramped by
this drought and everything it's..''
It's ok Red Jay!

{Obi shook me and looked at me sternly.}

……

"So maybe we defiled the Agorean alter!!!" …

''Maybe we ***** ******* on her a little son...''

(e said as I looked up at him)

Knell!

''But it's a "Genesis" Red Jay!'' Obi said wiping his eye

A genesis?

Yea Red Jay, Absolutely.

Now even Agora's drunken-lame will be more rational than a bloody Nile bugger!!

(e looked at me coldly)

''There's nothing less complicated then a King Red Jay.''

(I was horrified by t¶is illogical aphorism)

''Guess whooo ¿'' He said shaking his finger back

and forth at the window;..

then turning his tactical gaze toward me again.

''Sorry bud,'' He winked. °

''I have zero compassion in me for that..

cosmic_* whore hoarder PJ;'

Or for what happened to him on top of the inveterate Headless Triangle.'''

Knell.

You manna know why?

Why Obi?

''Because Red Jay,''

It's impossible to have success without women.

And before the Event;

It Was possible to have women who were intoxicated by another man.

But now that that villainous Great Horned Owl 'PJ' is out of

the picture;…

"Now,"

In addition to all those indispensable women we've already awed….

The flew_d woman who were extremely impressed

6

by how we waxed P.J. the Agorean ''Sicar;..¥
''Now even our enduring offspring will desire
us!''
Behold,.. My Isl justice' is never futile Red Jay.
.....

So your saying n|we can systematically produce
more cosmic wo,man through introversion?'' N:)
And we're clearly in better position with these of
ours
already, ..
Knell.
"Those curious girls who were possibly possessed by
what we did on top of the Headless Triangle??''
''O yea;'' said Obi
Daddy likes broken wings.....
Daddy likes it when they need my futuristic
wisdom.' √
"Now I remember." said Red Jay cracking a
smile
'Δ bad girl now is a bad girl later…
...
"& a l_ Agorean big girl now??"
..

[e was looking at me to finsh the black-line]]
The Ferrin's _| 'Agor_ean bad habit'??
"HaHa; easy there mister; e said
"It might take some time after that 'blood
curler;....
(all_extravagant)
[Obi said picking up his binoculars]
.....But I get it Red Jay; ''
(He said peering through)
I know the Agorean Horse-Whisperer sounds
,ideal
bud;.....
"I mean just to experience thiss stifling f
turpitude Red Jay;..."
....the chaos.
"But let's just say...."
Lets just say for now we're winning Von-
Isotropous's l_ platonic

war... ''
Knell.

.....

"I've got my eyes on a couple survivors as *we speak."
"Ya, I was afraid you might say that."
"Don't worry about the drought Red Jay,..." e said eye balling me.

.....

Maybe we should just keep our minds on the Sabbath
for a while;......
(e said gazing out the window...))
"I was thinking about making it 3 'big-boy days' instead of
1."
That's nice Obi.
Knell.

.....

"You manna know what the first deadly sin is Red Jay?_"
"What;"
"Having Sol-Adder faith & loving to zin???" ¿
;]
"I like it."
(e said looking through hiss binoculars)
But no; not me at least;...
"I've had my Sol-Adder faith today to."
I've had my faith like getting ;¿ poison Ivy.
"Pshh; " I laughed
What is it then???
"No,"
This isn't about abusing Sol-Adder faith,
or misleading people with no expectations Red Jay...
(Obi said looking at me like a little cannibal)
''This is about bowing."
What! "No way!"
(/e responded like a dragon fly) "Porous ArtE' you futile coon!!!" " Today <z> will be under no such curse!! _!!!

Knell!!!!

...

"Noooooo,"

T^hat's not what I mean Red Jay.

(Obi shook his head)

"Look;" he said softly

I'm not like blaming you for everything,or going
to burn you or anything,....

"behold,"

But Shaun the goshawk told me an interesting
little secret about you today....

"No, No, No Red Jay," [he said shaking his l
mission finger

again...]

"Did someone forget their little adrenal bow to
Isotropous this morning??"

Really??

[...said Red Jay who felt embarrassed about
getting (unofficial ly) c]aught not bowing to La

"Come on now bud, you know what they say;"

(e said repeating the goshawk's riddle)

"It's easy to throw a parade for yourself when
everything's going good;.."

But it's hard to be thankful when everything
comes crashing down on you...

(Obi said sounding very disappointed)

.....

"Or, I guess in some cases the other way
around;"...

(e said referring to the similar evil of both "pre-
P.J."

supplicators

When preying to Almighty God;..

Or with 'back[c up against the wall'

"petty little(s) petitioners."]

But in any case Red Jay,..

You know the rules.

"Sorry Obi."

"I'm trying to cultivate a godly dharma around
here Orenstein…"

....

"Red Jay, I am physically trying to pull the sword
of ecstasy from the stone around here in
Agora....
"Ya, the last frontier if you fuck with Agora."
(said
Red Jay eagerly)

..

"Famous-Talking-Owl will leave ae mon
famously lef_t oooo."

...

"Once a heathen always a heathen Red Jay',"
"What but a true conquerer conquers even the
most average of these l inappropriate_
appetites?
All who trust in his own elemental insignificance
would be
without vice!
Forsooth!
Lest they make their final mistake with the Obi.

.....

(I nodded)
Knell!
"And as far as men & women go,"
[Obi continued]
"So far as we need them,."
and needn't lie to ourselves anymore like too_
excoriated-headed atheists trying to address
{control) the economy:"
... <z>

...

,,,.Or someone poor.. <z>
"trying to winter our uxorious (help-permitted)
thirst by doing our
heroic deeds...
''And they need us;"
Hungry women with _l soul power ...
And therefore be not found shirking around the
hot flames and nicknames of other camps.
Physically there but in 2 places at once....
''Yes;"
Well said ¿ Hidalgo.

"No!!"

Behold!

"By the first d(o)boo'mon blue-moon Red Jay,..."

[¿]

"By the n|ext Agorean blue-moon you and <z>
should have

more bad-ass [l] Ricos between the two of us,

than every gleaming lion in Riverdale(z) _ eyes
when

the sun goes down.

Knell.

''And twice as many slaves as 2 Excaliburs!''

"Patroclus Red Jay." Obi said putting his arm
around me.

(I laughed)

Sound good killer???

Ha;

"O; so is that what it does?"

Haha Forsooth Red Jay!

You should see one of those Sol-Adder women
in heat!

Hypnotic?..

(Obi nodded his head)

"It's pathetic Red Jay."

Before 'The Event' they ruled the entire
ec(o)system.

But yea;

Those little pubic fly-traps of theirs can get
wetter then a water buffalo...;

''Ya,''

And spread out like a Hippo if you're not
careful...

Ha

Ya,

"And harrier than an iguana."

(said the twin as they burst into laughter..)

Olympia; Origins...:

Following the execution,... ^

The horrification on top of the Headless
Triangle,..

The sin that was still being exaggerated
by the look of this_l_stalking pandemic;...
(daily)
"The brothers recognized that Agora was going
to require more indian_women."
700' females down the dharmic drain because
of
are
soci(o)logical guidance;
And are instincts were instructing us to move on
from Agora quickly.
''The will of God is that we need to move on
to
fertile soil Red Jay;''
Forsooth,
It's time to let the stallion go.
"It's time to let the stallion go colonize." !!
(e said repeating the afterlife idiom..)
''That sounds good Obi,''
I need to get these Agorean women out of my
system...
(Obi was looking at his Atlas Map) 3
"Come here Red Jay;" he said motioning me
over von the round table to his jackal ° ream.Δ.
''Check out the Obi's gameplan.''
(Obi had a very_ '''sainer than dessert-bush look
on his face.
Behold!''''''' L
(Obi had circled Olympia.)
The Astrologers' Pact Red Jay. He said nodding
his head
at me<z>
''Behold,''
''I heard all of those informal women were on
strike
against
you and the <Z>_ Headless Triangle for what
happened to P.J.'s family.
Sorry Red Jay,...
e said like the grand |_anguage of Jared the
Agorean sky prophet

"According to Obi's Aquarius"
It all adds up... &
Obi, those women over there in Olympia are
twice as greasy as our little Agorean woman..
"And don't they already have a 'phantom-
emphasizing chief presiding???

..
..Know what I mean??.
...[(Obi stopped to think for a moment)
(Then shrugged his shoulders)]
"Maybe you're right Red Jay,...
Maybe the leadership over there is too strong to
be_
nosily interrupted by a couple of duesh bags..
(Immediately Red Jay felt uncomfortable about
how the Obi had worded his wisdom)
'' But you know what Red Jay,'' Obi said taking a
deep breath
We've lost 700 indian_women to that Agorean
grammy
winner P.J......
"700's godly w]omen to that black stallion."
So unless your method for manhood isn't as
work_ably
fucked as mine is;.......
(Red Jay nodded)
We gotta take Olympia down Obi.
We gotta take big-dick women down.
Wise words Red Jay;
Wise words,
....
But a little cherries not a little cherry
until it's on top of Obi....
"Once a virgoan always a virgoan bud."
......
"Obi, do you think we'll even have anything in
common with these...
You know;..
Unscratched Olympian women???
i guess either Olympian woman are a must,
Or they're not Red Jay.

"The real question is will a woman be patient
with a man who is in love."
(Said Onyx coming into the room)
"Hey Onyx."
I like your wisdom. Obi said {u} ¿
"The powers o _f r Agorean feminismm."
(Romance)
Red Jay said
aloud
...The sol teaching of 'Boolean the indian child..'
..
"But how can a woman even become a goddess'
Red Jay
????? (He) said ignoring the sentimental input
Pssh. How Obi.
Look at Me!
"Behold Red Jay don't you get it???
"Im the missing key!"
Our declarative link^ !
A God!
(We all laughed)
Now you know Red Jay!

..
"Your interpretation of relaxation doesn't offend
me.'"
......
"

—
"The woman who becomes like a man, is like a
fellow who becomes like a lion." said Onyx
"Ya, and what could be more repulsive than a
women who's repulsed by a God?" asked Obi
pshh. scoffed Red Jay
"And if she doesn't honor Obi's presence Onyx,
than that's what the Headless Triangle is for."
"Behold." Obi continued walking over to the
window,
....
...It was never really in me to become a precious
grandfather one day Onyx,....
Even a 'man' Red Jay;....,¿

Honestly, the only thing I've ever been
concerned about since I was a kid was Woofa-
like
immortality;... §^^
""A vvile sea-creature that cannot be conquered!"
....
"A blood so royal we're all offended."
(e said acting as if he was releasing a
dove back to heaven)...
/ \

....
But you know what,?.....

....
'Right now over there;_
Right now over there in choo Olympia Red Jay,...
Those 700' girls ;...
Those 700 women know where they belong,...
"They know where they belong like aa falcon
who
delivers mail on a regular basis."
(He said flailing his royal pinky ring)....
Forsooth!

...
Bravely spending out the remainder of their
days naked
underneath the copious spell of the Sphinx back
at the Headless Triangle...

...
A Obj yammic_continuity paradigm.
(I shook my head)
''Knell Red Jay,''
"The 3 of us have a grotto meeting' tonight with
Neptune the Agorean sea turtle."
"Onyx;".
We leave tomorrow for Olympia;,,
Agoras unholy right now.....

Elephant O'donto...:
"The following day we all got situated.."
Red Jay, Onyx, and I; on top of Neptune's hat-
like back

To corporately begin (r^)oceanic vantage_to
Olympia.' &

...

...

..."That's it."
That's a coelacanth right there...

..

"They never come up unless it's gent Obi.". (!)
They're" investigative mercenaries Red Jay."
...Behold
"As long as w*e don't have any triadic influences
along the way, if you know what I mean,..
W*e should be there by morning.''
Said Neptune speaking about Poseidon, the
messenger destroying God
of the Sea;
Well if I know Poseidon's trident, said Obi
"The last thing he's going to want is for any of
us to get lucky over there in Olympia !.
Red Jay laughed;
''How' is your half-Asian painting of Poseidon
going
Obi??
''Shhhhhh.''
''Low and behold Red Jay.'
(Obi had been painting something beautiful' A
picture picture of a
White Tiger
Lying down in the hills one evening
With a Chinese lantern blowing in von_the
background)
"And now you have _illuminated the perfect
plea_* for it!!!
''''

Behold a (r quiltless Poseidon!!!

...

''The n_lewd God of the Deep!!!_
Awesome Awesome. [said Onyx shaking his
head
But yes Red Jay, the work is diminishing as
usual;...

"I'll be done soon hopefully.
(Knell.)
-
"\Mr. Lucy belongs with hiz l_* 'black-sublimist'
allies."
<Z>
(Neptune permitted in a warning tone)
[]:
...
"So we had all arrived safvely off the shores of
the
Olympian empire,..
The sacrificial mecca‖ for the entire world.
Back in those times, Agora was still only a
emerging capital.
But still the only contemporary republic to
Greece!
Knell! said Obi trying to pump us up [] after
standing under the unfair demonstration_s
"We didn't leave Agora so as one day to
become precious grandfathers !!!"
Precious grandfathers like the spurious
Poseidon!
We imperiously left Agora
to obtain 'too many foreign wives' for ourselves!
"Behold the back of our water animal;" shouted
Obi
*It's the 3 contemporary wise men of Nazareth
who were not in
denial!"
I don't do good deeds! Obi shouted
''I live my life with zero animosity!''
Onyx do you approve of Obi's iffy wisdom?
asked
Red Jay
Onyx shook his head : {>
None of us had ever even been to Greece
besides
Onyx;'.
But as soon as we
arrived in ° Moolin.¶

As Neptune slid us up to the rocky shores}....
..
We knew this was God's country!!"
Knell.
We were greeted by several Olympians on
horseback,
Olympian men...
''Hello Onyx.''
Hello Paris.
Mono-zone Olympians were normally r_very
peaceful;..'
But at the same time very strict about
Non citizens having moccasin-autonomy over
here.
....Hidalgo knew we needed to clear the air
before we started circulating. Δ
Onyx stepped off,..
And went over to this Paris guy
to discuss us staying a couple nights here in
Olympia.
"What do you think they're talking about Obi?"
You say _qi we say chi Red Jay;...
....
Damn, Look how holy Paris's beard is!
I know; he has very fairy tale hair doesn't he.
......
Obi, you don't think they/re going to treat us
with formal
respect for a few days, and then like kill us or
something do you?"'
Obi??
This is really beautiful Red Jay,
"Look at the two pleni-potentiaries."
said Obi after the two respective republics; k
Agora and Olympia
smiled and shook hands.
"Seems like everything went pretty smooth."
"Smooth as Agorean adultery Red Jay."
....
"Pshh"
he laughed;

"I don't know private."

...

"Paris said Mer-Chi finds none of us guilty of
anything unholy!"
Said Onyx coming back over to us.
Guilty for what ??? asked Obi
He finds none of us guilty for trespassing into
God's country!
''Behold,''..
He said you two can do whatever you want over
here in Olympia.
"Just so long as you don't eat from the tree of
life!
Eat from the tree of life, or even touch it lest
you_literally
die!!
Haha, that's funny Said Obi
"Just wait for the serpent; ;s offor."

...

"Lightning ready Aries.",, <ser>¤
()

...

"You know what Red Jay,"
"I think I'm really starting to like this guy."
''I like the way he formally mounted his steed.'''
said Red
Jay
''Obi," said Onyx
The blameless chief of Olympia,
The Great Mer-Chi,
Would like to meet with you tonight to go over
some concerns.
What the fuck Onyx!?
Concerns???
He said it has to do with all men;..
'& preferential women in veils Obi,...
That's all I know.
''Up," said Obi immediately after;
I just solved the experimental r_iddle Red Jay,
Haha.
All of these sexy Olympian woman over here

are like Mer-Chi's granddaughters.
"I sure hope he knows I'm literally qualified to bend one of these Olympian
hot-tamales over like a step child..... (e was thinking) Tau}
"Its Mer-Chi's birthday today." said Onyx
His 11th birthday.
"Really."
"Yep, he's the guy," said Onyx
Apparently after Diaphanous's voodoo
(/_\tales) crescent concept e reincarnated
into a young vampire."
Jesus Christ!!!
He reincarnated as a vampire?!!
Oh my gosh Red Jay!
"They're going to make us straight vascularly-protrusive with holy
water
and then suck (r brains out!" Obi mocked
///\\\s a styled; cool-addicted yoyouth at the cemetery
[...
Where and when do I need to be for this little meeting Onyx?
''The Bear.''
The Bear???
"Tau-Manias!!!"
That's the most famous romp in the world Orenstein.
Tau Maniacs. said Red Jay
...
''Extreme wisdom date. (scorpio+
...
Paris said you won't miss him,...
Just b*e there by 8.
"Mer-Chi and his uxorial entourage will b*e traveling by way of
'Y '[Agorean-Fox-Skull]_n..<Z>
Damn", I need to find one of those.
"Nope,.. No way Mr."
"Just humble yourself for everyone please.'"

I do not want to end up as dead vampire pussy.
"Vampire fools gold Red Jay." $

...
...(Onyx and I both looked up> at eachother...)
[...

...
I'm sure vampires are probably just a
persuasive myth around here..
A persuasive myth to protect the beautiful
Olympia.
Knell;
Like a mysterious scarecrow or something.
Its not a fucken myth<Z> said Onyx
Forsooth.
So we did some century scouting around in
Olympia for a little
while
until it was time for Obi's meeting with Mer-Chi.
Now Olympia was a little n_vein for a needy o
spirit,..
No place for the spacious wildebeest to stomp.
But apparently, even +he Agorean superficiality
was still nothing in
comparison
To what was going on inside Mer-Chi's pyramid.
Mer-Chi had explained to Onyx that because
of the lavishness of his household;
It would be impossible for Mer-Chi to be taken
seriously;
And also that no one besides him can even
enjoy it,...
That's why he invited Obi to chill with him in his
sedan for a little while;..
Just to finally hang out and go over some
concerns.
The three of us were there waiting for him and
his clan
When they decided to show up...
Knell.

..
''All of a sudden;;;.'' <'a terrible omen fell

obversely

over the land as the local caravan approached;'.

''..no of us Agoreans could go back to the grave.. ''

...

...

...

''Everyobe appeared to be courageously
harboring some
sort of savage ghost.... !) !)
Behold;;...
'4 Olympian men were carrying Mer-Chi \
around in his little mobile rocking chair.........
''nd no one lay was allowed to get any higher
than
a nested craw-fish... <Z>
"Don't wander off you two," said Obi before
stepping inside
''Safety in numbers.''
You don't look so good Obi..

.....

Seriously?
Serious as a snake bite Ob.
Onyx said you haven't slept in weeks because
pf what happened on top of the Headless
Triangle...
You know,
After the perverted thing that happened to Mer-
Chi.
"What are you talking about Red Jay\:?"
(Then in a moment,...
One vaguely conspicuous moment in time like a
l pharaoh's first comet...)
"Hey special."
'There I was,'...
An inexperienced holy boy, toe to toe/aw with
the
King of Agora,...;
Everything around me felt so coincidental.
So practical that my mind couldn't process it.
I was about to pee my pants;,,
Then,

like drifting off to sleep and slipping into a fucking
nightmare];...
It all made undeniable sense;;;..'<>''''
Pacing Jaguar???????
Oh my god he lives!
Son of a bitch!!!!
(But there was nowhere safe to run...)
''Pacing Jaguar isn't my name anymore Obi,''
Because personally I have conquered death.''
I was just staring at him with my mouth open.
P.J.,
The God of Olympia,
H
d dressed himself in all gold & leopard. &
….
He looked like a vicious vamp!
"I like your houses and your streets."
Said Obi who was totally at a loss for words.
[[But Mer-Chi was so far minded
that everything I said felt like hubris.ll
"Please don't kill me Mer-Chi!!!"
Behold!
"The Headless Triangle is my idol!!!!"
((said Obi starting to confess his sins))
"As a matter of fact Gold and Leopard are my
idols also!!!"
'Shhhhhh.''''
(Trying to perceive Mer-Chi was almost like
looking into a melted_spoon,... <Z> .
...
ThE Obi just knew rhat he was probably about to
unhumiliate himself...)
"God." said Mer-Chi peacefully <z>
((And that \ scientific 'nomen'' alone by itself,......
Was pretty mucx the end of Mer-Chi's speech.))
So you think its ok that I embarrassed you like
that?
''I accept you Obi.''
"I know." said Obi who had started to cry
Mer-Chi handed me a jiff, (peace pipe)

"Here."
How do you handle so many women Mer-
Chi???
(I said through the tears)
How do you have meaningful relationships with
all of them.??
I know it's unusual; he said
"Behold,"
"What goes down in Mer-Chi's is just common
nature to us."

....

"All of those women are forward rock-stars," e
said
"They love their autonomy."
Pssh, I love their anatomy.
"Wow,"what could be more fun?? I thought to
myself
They're all vampires;... he said sternly
You wouldn't even be attracted to them
anymore
if you knew how evil Mer-Chi was!
Haha; once a heathen always a heathen.
"crucial emotion." he said
...Haha
"So how do we move forward from here Mer-
Chi;" I asked
How can I ever repay you!!
"Behold!" said Obi
1,000,000 talents of" lauded ser!!!
"Stop." he replied
Mer-Chi doesn't need gold.
Or 2,000,000 talents of Obi silver,...

......

I need you to set m*e free for the next million
years Obi.
Forsooth.
I need to be at the permittable place on
the earth.
"At_the r l / \ sexy place on the earth for the
beginning
of time."

"The beginning of time??"
"Im in love(o with Olivia Obi,..." Mer-Chi
continued
But I hate this damn place.
(said Mer-Chu referring to his little space man
cocoon...)
Forsooth!!
"Mer-Chi you're going to feel like Jefferson in
the
land of Jefferson!!!!" e said
You, and all 700 of your obsequious women!!!!!
Knell,
And then the King wept afterwards;..
Because of what happened to everyone
when Obi tried to eat from P.J.'s tree of life...
[<Z>
Origin: The rattle-sake_text
''So in talking with Mer-Chi;''
W*e had agreed to have the Agorean Empire
specifically positioned;
Filially stratified for the upcoming "ground
moon."
Which; according to Him;
Was supposed to b*e a great day inspired by ''the
affairs of the
Gods.''
The important culmination of roughly seven
eons;.. (wonders)
Knell,
The sol_annex of Agora to Olympia meant that
Mer-
Chi would take the West;
And that the Obi would take the East.
Knell,
''The important part of Agora where the
Headless
Triangle still breaths...
And for them all to until ''The ¿ Fall;''...
To get along in a moπe he_numerical working
environment.
The night Pacing-Jaguar returned home;

Represented ceremonially by a docile-h King-
Cobra that was unwilling to bite;..
Then once again by a child sneaking up von
_'the
snake from behind;
''Intending to finally capture it;…''
A more significant dance
That symbolically described the incapacity for
anyone
To understand the formal veneration of this holy
day,...
The one that had been described to me by Mer-
Chi.
----Expressed by the false;
un>able to actually see eyes of the cobra.
Explaining that even though his people haven't
quit trying to logically
prepare for this day for so long; Remaining very
aware but relatively fearless
for the last t(r|y housand years;.. ''That even now;''
Knowing that the day is only weeks away;..
''Just weeks away from the the peerless devil's
charade...
It was still just as impossible to mentally
prepare
for.'
'But anyhow, upon his return;
The Great Mer-Chi;…
The Obi still thought that even though it might
be ll futile;..
It was still probably for the best that he launch
the Peacock Δct.
The motley - facetious act commemorating
the official return of Mer-Chi----Otherwise little
known
as the planetary leadership of God.
''Don't worry Red Jay.''
''When you attempt to pave the way for a thing;
you at least prove you're a emissary.'' <z>
...Mer-Chis a little bit more eccentric than our
jiffing Agorean forefathers. (He) said fishily

...

"Yaa,.. I can definitely see how expecting such a promising
change in rreality
could cause everything besides a ¿ voss
& a
bloody mary to all be pretty futile. ^

..

Pretty??
Just laugh at ourselves {;Daddy} Red Jay,
"Just laugh at y(|our l_ self pending self<"
You'd probably be ae fidgety// night-hawk if
you really
knew what was good for you..
You know?

..

Behold,
"Yea<z> guess the corporate demension f
mother-nature should literally end up
being a l modest creation after all;,,"
'And 'that lawless d****' father-time, a extremely
clever one.'
''Awesome beaver shit hud'' (Obi said looking up
at the heavens)
""""""How could you ever estimate as good as it
possibly
gets???""""""
You really can't Red Jay;..
"O_r I guess you just did."
"It really is completely futile to try and stomach
'comming to grips' with Olympia Obi?"
"I guess the only difference between this and
common fear is
that I would have to ob_viously believe it."
All we can do is be interested Red Jay;
"All a couple of l lawless day-killers like us can
do
is be (a) l interested.''
'But I'll tell you what is w futile,..'
Is trying to stomach a women¿ ho never worries
but always worries.

"You know," a woman who makes you smile so
big you need to run away Red Jay??

...

"O,"

..<Z>s a woman the only quantifiable (p.o.)
antithesis to a modest creation in the e_ntire
universe???

In that, a beautiful women really may help us
map-out God's limit to all of creation?

"That the matter is really pretty' black and
white??

"The all_ watchful eye of Von Isotropous." Obi
agreed

'black girls and Yang girls.'

"Ya Red Jay,"

Out of everything that you would most likely,
real;ly ever

see out there,

In the whole negative _universe,.. <Z>

That whatever this beauty;... Forsooth,

Whatever tHis...opposite,.. e)ssentially

illuminated sol of a true Agorean goddess is,…

That that is the that that for the equivalency of
God's

optimized perfection.

Yes, as far as I'm actually concerned.

I expect physical affection too,.

The man of your dreams Red Jay??" said e

Obi brushing his arm

....

(Then we both sat there_ r_or a moment,...

Knowing we couldn't exactly cope with a life
of /

being serious with a woman...)

Much to the confidence of boarding sailors...

You know Red Jay;...

As a on-behalf_factually impressed prisoner of
Almighty God,

I have chosen to embrace this l celestial
imprisonment. O?

The perfect balance of Isotropous is really

leering bud;..
And all we really know,...
Is that the unofficial Tau of this Earth,…
Is not the true,_eternal Tau God has wholly intended
for the Universe;.. (Chi)...
Its like the magicness of the thing that is a complete fact of magic is totally missing right now.

...

It's like a human body without the eyes Orenstein...
......a sleeping cobra.
Knell. said Obj in remembrance of the Sesquatchi
(|
''In manna (y ways our l_ planet is just a c)reative
abomination.''
(Red Jay laughed to himself thinking about the ''cobra dance.'')

……..

"But according to Mer-Chi there is about to be a magical evening blowing in."
A terrible evening we have both been personally chosen to experience.
That [l] perfidious deal responsible for this Rhode Island draught we've been experiencing…
The when of all whens Red Jay.
E
Well then what are we doing Obi?
Should we like go see the Grand Canyon or something?
TheLov'aura Canal??''
No way Red Jay;
"We're about to witness Mother Nature's bosom!"
I'm about to return as a gorgeous mountain man with pupils the ying of olives & cheek bones the size of gourdes!
What the fuck could the 7 wonders of this

fucken

(¿) trans-omni place prepare me for?

a jiff full-circle,... (X) "........."

All we can do; is point-out the blessings of our gift until the end Red Jay;

Thankful for thu_unequaled day that has basically been an

annual

'end of the Moon-Serpent Party in Mer-Chi's culture for

the last couple 'thousand years.

Forsooth.

(...Red Jay was looking at his reflection in the glass.)

''Man, I can't imagine transfigurating Obi.''

You know,..

Transforming into an Agorean angel.

(He laughed)

....trampling shit like a rag-doll

(e looked on proudly)

"Fate is the end, and destiny is a beginning Red Jay."

When life ends it's your show.

A superconcious bald-eagle in the sanctuary of God!

The beasts of all beasts!

But you know what Red Jay??

If Mer-Chi's death has taught me anything to weigh it's this....

...

It's that that, cool little reflection you see in the mirror everyday

will always just be a guy in the glass...

"No matter who you are."

(Obi stopped for a moment)

But your the patriot Red Jay,...

The patriot with all the zeal.

Knell was a yesterday goddamnit!

And albiet Red Jay,

No matter what happens in life,...

You still have to find a way to admire yourself at

the end of the day.
(Red Jay was feeling over the considerable
bones of
his face.)
....
"Is it not already too late to sell all our
verners Red Jay?" (:vest)
Is it not too late to leave everything behind?
Would we not =just look like the frantic
neighbors who lost
out on their only attempt to gain Von
Isotropous's eternal
salvation?
You know, if we left,
or prostrated ourselves like a bunch of phonies
on top of the Headless
Triangle or something?
"Knell,"
''The social precedent of Agora has always been
wisdom Red Jay;''

...

'''Above everything extravagant Red Jay,''

..

''Above human rights and ae free-will.''
'''Above Goldkizm's common sense.''
'''Above mine and your friendship???
"Have we not founded Agora by ourselves with
our own two hands??''
''Obsequiously around the all to mysterious,
fulfilled will
of God!?''
''The filial will of God that has been a_for-devil's
only
sanctity!??
....
''This was our vison!
His vison for us!!!'' .....
''Have we not run everything unholy' off Red
Jay???
''The law is written on our Sol-Adder hearts Obi.''
''On our little Sol-Adder souls.''

....
Summed and perfected Red! !!!
We need a goal Obi.
A goal for Moolin, until Sublimest Naga's 'hot little returning.
/"\We should erect a sphinx!/"\
To be available Red Jay;..
To be available like a ealous zay, white horse for the big day.
……..I think that & our angels is probably the missing key to life's optimal puzzle.
Haha.
Sounds good bud.
I like your wisdom.
o Origins; Plan Shaanxi:
So according to the Night-Sun prophecy,...
The land of Agora was about to turn into ae butterfly.
Chosen out of all the other lands of the world,
As the place that theπ Gods would dramatically descend,
And that their only begotten children would apparently ascend.
But instead of what we had all heard, involving this precarious reality
Concerning the day and the hour,...
A 75% chance that it would happen on Rabbit day,
And a 50% chance it might happen on Wild Boar day,..
There was no cosmic transcending happening around Agora to speak of except for the occasional chap.
Obi's power point presentation about Orion's widow was a echumenical bust,..
And the expectant Sol-Adders were starting to get a little feisty about Agora not being chosen soil.
Mercy was Not on the king's mind, Mer-Chi, the actual God of Agora,..
Was turning mean as a snake!

And 'the native Agorean prince' Obi,
his prodigal son,
Was turning meaner than O'rion's widow.
''Use your wisdom Red Jay,''
There's not goanna be any holy
commemoration in this fucken town!
I mean, what's another fucken billion years at
this point.
''Sad, but true.'' Red Jay replied foully
Suck it Red Jay!
Pity practically makes that fussy comment a
conclusive reality!
Forsooth;
But instead of pretending I'm not a god;..
Rather than the folly of absolute denial,....
I'm going up to lay down on top of the Headless
Triangle for awhile,...
I'm going to lay down like the journeying Osiris
did,
Let go of the typical odds,
And see if I can't figure this whole thing out.
(Obi was on his way up to go analyze the
rhythm of the constellations atop the great
pyramid)
Jupiters in Leo Red Ja....
But then,.. after only going up a few stairs,x
. . . .
''Oh''
''My''
''Leopard.''
What is it Obi?
Red Jay,.. I know this might sound kinda
objective,..
But I think I just figured out my entire life's
purpose,...
What is it???
Well,. have you ever heard of that 'all inclusive'
barbeque phrase,...
"The more the merrier, if there's a inaugural
Hollywood contest?"
''Yes.''

Well as a matter of fact Red Jay,..<z>
Lest it merely be the eerie will (von)
a fire breathing puff of the sulfureous Saint
Nick,....
'<Z>' may be able to make it a transcendental/y
exclusive Mon.." /!\
How so Obi??
"Behold,"
So who's got more l arithmetical prodigies
tucked in_for TAP;
& ready to ascend the cultless abyss than
Shaanxi Red Jay?"
(Obi paused) You know Red Jay,....
Its only........
Luck??
(Obi said raising his eye brows)
"Haha."
"I am going to use young Tim as my example!!"
"One who is surpassing in disparity!"
evl
''Bon fire Red Jay??''
"Haha, you're such a fool Obi."
e
said barely imagining the\ pl\urality
"I know,"
"I am about to send r great friend; & legendary
obit-healer Loo-Loo;...
that ol Sol-Adder stiff a concerned e-mail."
(Said Obi going down the stairs this time......)
"I just need to eat a tart first."
... /
(Loo-Loo was the r) unofficial <I>nculcating
father of orient_ancient
Asia.
Oriental pole-cat &A tru ly permanent holy
man...'')
Forsooth!!!!
(LLlves mostly reclusive because of hiss
tempting smile... :)
"'Don't forget their beautiful presence of
formal respect

Obi."
"The presence h_ood Red Jay."
"The beautiful aura of h_ood."
"Dear Loo;"
I hope you are doing well.
It has been such a long time since our last talk
about 'vast not being an idle!'
Your wisdom has given me hope & peace on my
journey...
A little bird on my shoulder!
You are a fountain of culture Loo!!
And as a matter of fact,
A important sign from God has come into my
mind today about this very same thing!
He has given me understanding about the
coptic puzzle of my 'facsimile' world,
And a funny riddle about his favor_ite people in
the universe!!
''With your permission Loo,''
Agora would like to come function a l
rap9ture_ _*
in Shaanxi this Christmas!
My last initial visit to Shaanxi was too short,..!!!
Although you sure did enlighten me!!!...
''''The Tau is God's puppet.''
''And those who follow the Tau are God's
buddies.''
So as I was saying Loo Loo,..
''Can we come celebrate the stimulating day with
a little
diversity this Chirstmas??''
Like some 'chi' entitied,. o.p. carrier Agorean's,
And also how the interesting people
von_Shaanxi do it???
''A radical bon-fire, with all the people
celebrating
humility & peace with the dragon bones???''
(gallism)
A God n Shaanxi Loo-Loo...
Embarrassed on his perch. Δ

..

Knell!

This Christmas Satan will still be King-choo Loo.

---Obi

P.S.

I still think Agorean idolatry is awesome!"

Dear Obi,

I am so happy to hear you have taken control of
your compulsive desires!

To be proud of where we are from is something
very natural,

But we must understand that obsession is something
superfluous,..

And by nature unhealthy.

Where I am from is something sacred to me as
well Obi,

& I also believe that God has brought us all to a
single point in time as you do,..

Making the confluence of our two cultures all
the more expedient.

Our inevitable union is indeed a masterpiece
Obi!

''Out of all the stars in the sky Obi;'' not one sign
of an

imposter!!!

There can never be too many 1 Sol-Adders!!!...

You cannot squeeze juice out of a little seed my
son,...

But you can squeeze the juice out of a ripe
piece of fruit!

--Loo

P.S. Zero Idolaltry!!!!

]

...

I

s that a yes Onyx?

The bon fire was a great idea Obi.

You've inspired a selfless change in me.

Some people are hens, some people are
phoenixes Red JAy,...

I'm not reallysure what we would have done if
Loo and I hadn't been all_in for thE regular-

friendly air convention this year.
Saw entire/ly eye to "anti-eye" about thaT off-
ensive X pillage..
''With that being said though,''
Even though I'm not really worried about it,..
I'm not exactly sure what the hell all that
overly<z><z>
obsessed with Agora stuff was all about;..
....
"There's nothing wrong with a hen Obi."
But you know what they say, about that
ol farmer who keeps on yoking the ox….
Sometimes that l philosophy of yours can get
(a)   l
out of hand.. £i (reap)
"There's a philosophy karma at the core of
Boolean's teaching Red Jay."
Besides,..
Everybody knows tha witches brew is always
just right!
Nevertheless. said Onyx
This eternal event is ob_viously much bigger
than
Agorean philosophy,..
''This is about ae reunion.''
That's right Onyx,
We all come from the same bull.
"Too much pride is absolute ignorance," Onyx
continued
_The decedents of plague, (gravity)
Rather than all the l funny children of one
Heavenly
Father.''
(Red Jay laughed,..)
(And then started playfully sizing up Obi)..
Knell.

....

"No pearl is sharp."
(Onyx said kneeling down to pick up a rock)
"What can even a good man contribute to
the earth, who

is not even r[eally ae genuine one."
..../

...

''The Headless Triangle has never murdered
anyone as an example.'' Said Obi
No champions. said Red Jay
No winners! said Obi

....

''The thing no one likes to ever talk about.'' said
Onyx

.....

Ya,..
I guess someone better go enlighten Mer-Chi...
......Yaa

...

'A man's' wisdom is pure,.'
But r ation can be impetuish,... Δ
'Sometimes wΔ can be very inspiring,'
But sometimes u cn be very unoriginal,
''You want to connect cultures_v and enjoy
exploring.''
"But who or what could actually make you happy
but God!
Knell.
''Or should you continue to look for what you
have already found??
"What on earth can f_foil or galvanize God???

..

''A scorpion coming after his own crown is not
common sense.'''

..

"Your gang's one interest right now is for one
valuable
mission!'''
To uproot a l blasphemy!!
"But what you are really actually pursing is
parting from
your urban life,.." (beneficial)
''So even if you
go hunting far and wide you shell never
escape!!

You wil not beat this evil presence of what
is annoying you..._
"If love does not exist love does not exist.
Δ
''Now love is a mystery.''
....
(Then a) l green camillion shimmied his way out
the window)
....
"What a Von." (!}

..
((Red Jay was hawking his brother with a very
evolved grin...))
"Sol-Adders don't jump the gun when there still
in the leaves." [He said]
(Obi looked up with a humorous look on his
face)
.....
"Mer-Chi's right Red Jay;... W*e can't leave
Agora."
.....I was beginning to think I was Zing Zing or
something.
I think so too Obi,
It is never wise to disassume _ patients.
Even if it feels like you need to sail to Shaanxi
sometimes.
"But you know when you want something really
bad Red Jay,"..
And all you can think about is having that one
_thing,..?
And because of all the impending excitement,..
Everything else besides that one _difficulty
becomes sorta,.. ya know
The end of the yellow brick road seems sorta...
motif????
Yea,..
And the only thing that would actually enable
you to deserve
that one thing is that one fricken thing??!!
U huh,
A 2 wala.

Yea Red Jay,...
A damn 2 wala...
Obi, it's going to take
a Hell of a magician to get this thing done.
I haven't felt so much as a damn trimmer.
I haven't felt so much as a titillation!
You can 'save the world' all you want. said
Onyx
"But you can't take a shortcut on love."
....
(The two brothers looked at each other)
....
Listen to my wisdom.
Once upon a time;
There was a boy named Coco-Tan who lived in
the city of Tenchoi.
Out of all the sons of this great city;
No one loved Allele more than Coco-Tan.
---The Indian princess of Tenchoo.
Allele was asleep between the hanging
gardens;
Awaiting the day that one of the sons of
Tenchoi
could set her free with a kiss.
But only the right suitor could free her.
One whom was undeniable and she felt
comfortable with.
For Allele was more beautiful than heaven
itself...
Now Coco-Tan was not the pride of the land;...
But it was the King's son
Two-High-Mountains..
A fierce warrior who could not be killed in battle.
He did love Allele;..
But not above everything on the whole earth;
Not above everything on the whole earth as
Coco-Tan did.
For even though he was a pure spirit;
His love for her was not inconceivable.
Then,..
Suddenly one day;

Coco-Tan lost his sight!
......
But that would not stop him from either dying,
or awakening Allele with a kiss!
So then Coco-Tan followed the big river,
The river known as Albion.
''Because of my great loss; he thought
Even if I find her, I will be like a useless n*****!''
But then,+
He slipped into the river.
That's when Pisa, the God of Gods,
Turned him into a fish.
"Will I ever find her!" He asked Pisa
Maybe yes, maybe no.
But instead of begging him for more wisdom he
decided to take action!
Swimming all the way up-stream to Tenchoo.
"Now this thing is stopping me!" exclaimed
Coco-Tan
''Even if I was able to walk on the land;''
"A talking fish could never even stir the pot!"
Like this, I would never be anything more then a
friend,
"An unholy role that would make me
inconsiderable
as a romantic companion!"
So then Coco-tan asked the divine Pisa for help
again.
Behold,
''Now I have traveled for many days.''
"Please restore my hands and my feet so I can
go
out from the water and begin my destiny with
Allele!"
No,..
"Create me into something exorbitant!"
Exorbitant and Glorious!
Silence! demanded Pisa
Have I not already given you the good path!?
The path whereof you have not grown up
because of your hard walk?!?

Please! replied Coco-Tan
I have heard of your wisdom!
"But the spirit of my heart will be dead soon
If I can not go out of this water!"
''Then,'' after I do what I have in my mind to do,
I will be your slave forever !!! he begged
Or if you cant,.....
..believe it or not'_
<Z> will surly die from exhaustion!
Knell!
Do not ask me for anything else!
Then Pisa turned Coco-Tan into a flying-snake,
and ended all involvement with him.
"Well then, no more help from that old f rascal."
said
Coco-Tan who came out of the water.
"Now, since I have been created into something
good I can actually begin my life with Allele."
Now the whole earth was Kukulkan's!
All the jewelry and articles of gold!
But there was no gold, or any treasure that he
had really ever desired.
Even after the fact that he was allowed to go out
& dominate the whole earth like a king,....
His heart was still very heavy for Allele.
His only desire was for the day that Allele was
finally his.
"How shall I ever die!" yelled Kukulkan
screaming about hiss immortality
And now my name is befitting a beautiful
woman!
A woman who's beauty has tortured my soul for
a long time!
Then,..
After bowing to Pisa and thanking him for
everything,...
Coco-Tan flew to the end of the world!~
And finally kissed her.
.... "Hello Sweet Love."
"It is important to know that you are more beautiful
than Heaven itself."

"And now,"
I am your one true lover who has awoken you."
.....
Behold, she said
"You are not before or after any of my lovers."
she replied
Although she was still very tired.
So then finally,
The two lovers; Allele and Coco-Tan,..
Were finally really married!
---The End
.....(The two boys looked at each other rather
emotionally)
Just harden your heart Red Jay,...

....
''Just harden your native heart.''

Goldkizm bows to Kiyyun:
Then one day,
after playing "Na," the assertive wisdom game
Against four risky jack rabbits,...
We were all just off the dormant trail of Toyalti;
And there had had been a veridical statue
erected to Kiyyun;...
The highly esteemed god of the desert.
Obi went up to inspect "Kiyyun's descension to
earth;
But then Onyx came up and bowed to Kiyyun.
Obi laughed; and looked at Red Jay;
Red Jay shrugged.
God bless you Onyx!
Obi said reprimanding his idolatry;
Do not worship a dead stone!
Are you not aware that this prideless idol of
yours
is not the real Kiyyun
and only an illogical item that will surly perish!
Long live the aging eyes of the Headless
Triangle!!!

...
"How can an old rock be a hero Onyx." mocked

Red Jay
Onyx looked up angrily;
"Open up your minds you idiots."
Do you think that I think?
Or do you two assholes not know that only the
heart can make a gift holy???
Is this not just a sensible gesture to an ineffable
God who needs nothing?
Hypocrites!
(The two brothers looked at each other...)
Goldkizim's Paradigm:
So we continued on,..
A bit further down the trail until we ran into
another mysterious statue…
Look! said Obi
It's a veridical recreation of the Last Supper!
What a majestic boon of our Lord, and his
difficult fellows!
My personal acquiescence.. said Red Jay
That's the cardinal sin Orenstein.
(said Obi reprimanding his lack of faith)
I just manna know.
No. said Onyx stepping back.
This isn't a portrayal of Jesus,..
"This is ae ruin of Dionysius."
"The God of nadir and debauchery having a
feast among men."
Then immediately,Obi ran up to the sleazy
abomination,
And bowed low to Dionysius.
What are you doing Obi?!!! Red Jay yelled
If someone offers you the world you usually
have to give them something more in return!
The formal exchange for your soul is
irrevocable!
Don't worry Red Jay,
''I'm not selling my soul to Imphasus-Hedonism.''
…
Even though there's really nothing wrong with
''the philosopher's propriety...'^
"In that desire must master itself."

44

An forfeiting desire,... |r
(He paused)

.....

''May mean the soul of a talking fish,..''
Toying with the lust of Sheol....
.....(everyone looked at each other>:)
"Man, I feel sorry for Mer-Chi Obi."

..

(Ob looked at me strongly})
'''Vampires only come out at night Red Jay."

....

"Mer-Chis got all the day to crack the whip over
those little jalapenos."
Plus now he's got the trusty Agorean flag
keeping him safe.
....(Obi cleared his throat)
"But our dear friend Onyx is off here."

.....

Debauchery is a stigma.
O yea?
*The rights to wisdom means you're a formal
player does it not?"
Well, what do you mean by that O_bi?
I don't manna get myself a permanent thorn in
the flesh.
(Obi sighed)
Dionysus is not the God of ''inconcupiscent''
flamers Red Jay,...,
Dionysus is the God of culture. ..
A little pleasure is a must, & truthfully
God's ultimate favor..,
And as far as I'm concerned you idiots,...,
"The in_proverbial peacock is coming home to
roost."

...

"And I think we all know what that means!!"

....

"Blood-like intimacy amongst his little guys and
gals out here in Agora!!"

....

"The Puritans after a hopeless winter!"

You know what I'm sayin>?
(Obi paused)
C
orrect me if I'm wrong,.......
But everyone needs to devil in a
l
''culture culture.''
Identity.
Innocence.
"The marriage."
Like a young heart when it snows!

..

"Streets of gold,
And inked-up barbarians on the hunt for mire
diamonds!''
"Preppy school boys throwing roses at our feet
Red Jay."
Authentic Sol-Adders!
Agorean culture huh...
I think that may b*e all I need...
"That's all anyone needs." Obi continued
Mother nature is a taken poet already Onyx,..
But without us, for one, thriving in our natural
environment,..
Forsooth!

..

A l_carnivorous monk' slithering his way
through
the unknown _l Tree of Mastery ......

..

WE+ as perhaps the holy keys to mother
nature's divine impetus,..

...

Without that interesting law Onyx,...
without us thriving n (r) correct mono-culture
that is;..
Literally the meaning of life you guys,....
"Biters." muttered Onyx
The corollary of our existence would be like the
penultimate wrath of a illegitimate_crescent
moon... <z>

"Please."'' Obi said looking down at his watch
.....
Or the downright vexatious missing front leg of
a
3 legged bird dog...
Uncouth!

....
Ha (Obi smirked)
Have a Sol-Adder salad in remembrance of me
Red Jay?
A Soul-Adder salad???
(Then the brothers burst into laughter)

....
"And we all know my o fashion t_heory on that
monism
apparition."
((Obi continued between his laughter...)
"Red Oak 'the moon-do6' doesn't chase his tail
Onyx,..
But Johnnie dogs do...
But once you go double bird dog you can't
exactly fly
back. Said Red Jay
[''<>']
Yea, you can't let it go when you're alone. Said
Obi
Satan Obi!!!!!
(hahahahah...)
"Wow."

...
"That is wayy too Prince."
"Don't offend Tau."
ha.
too introductionary.

...
Not lairish enough for you Red Jay???
(Hahahahaha...)
"My God, your a phcyco Obi.

...
"Xiller instinct Bon."

...

"Sorry bud, I'm way too Leo."
Roll a 5 you hermit.

....
"The act takes too much body."
"Great."
Good cloths.
"Stop."
<Z>
"I don't want to talk about homosexuality." Onyx
said firmly
But I would like to revisit the premise of culture.
Listen to my wisdom.......
Once upon a time,...
In the land of Egypt,..
There was a young boy named Osiris.
Old enough to be an astronomer,
But too young to be a God.
He had a birthday coming up one year,..
And he was insightful enough to understand
that
he didn't want it to be arbitrary.
''What do you want for your birthday son?'' his
mother asked him
A new bed. He said
And a couple of bonnets.
His mother shook her head and begun to
spread the warning about Osiris's birthday party.
When the day arrived,...
And it came time for everyone to show their
grace to the boy,..
He was shrewdly shading himself by the Nile.
So everyone had a light heart that day about the
wisdom of O'siris
Making everyone join him at the Nile.
"I didn't expect to see so many Jews here!"
he yelled out as they approached.
"Don't comment on your mothers wisdom!"
Yelled
his father
Are you ready to open your presents??
No. he said. (sadly)

''Anything but a bed is unownable.''
And then everyone laughed to themselves
about the response of this precious little boy.
………………
Wow.
''What a genius at micro-sociology.'' . ..
"He created a culture with his wisdom didn't he
Onyx."
He didn't mean any harm with that Jew
comment.
Actually he was engendering a welcoming
brand of intimacy. Onyx explained

Ka''z Tokaomok l:
<|>
Obi was appalled by the young Osiris's
inconceivable wisdom;
And he was determined to model this renown
excellence.
Later that night,
The two brothers were back at home doing
crosswords.
''There's no good word for A.M.''. ...
…..Obi?
..
''Am I too much of a manic Red Jay???''
Yes?
Why what's wrong???
Well I've been thinking long and hard about 2
things Red Jay,..
What?
Hating the arbitrary,..
And loving the personal.
{}
We need to throw a party Red Jay,..
A real personal party.
Something not the whole world will be invited
too,
But something only us Agoreans will be invited
too.
The harvest is plenty but the workers are few

Red JAy.
(Red Jay laughed to himself)
But we need a theme,...
An impeccable paragon.
A nutcracker theme. said Red Jay practically
''Ya.'' He said in agreement with himself
Everyone's superstitious about nutcrackers....
Obi said thinking about the idea aloud
Ya,and stentorian black holes. said the latter
O my God it fits perfect Red Jay!
"With a glimmerous new age look!"
Mad hatter!
The B.J. Festival Orenstein!!!!
The B.J. Festival???
O my god that's Agorean.
Forsooth!!!
If ye made a promise ye made a promise!!!
....
The B.J. Festival!!!!!!!!!!!!!
Merely throwing (a) l obit party was simply not
the
tradition in Agora.
Once the sand doors were opened,
The guard of the Headless Triangle,..
You knew you were probably going to be
underprepared.
Obi was the dev\ious king of amusement,
And the corroborative Sol-Adders were in love
with the concept of dressing up
like a band of smitten hooligans for the ying_
insulting B.J. Festival.
Inside the pyramid that night was like being
inside of a clam,..
The halls lavishly decked in nebular blues.
Hello Obi.,
Hello Orenstein.
Red Jay you look like the fuzz of the Emerald
City.
Obi you look like Henry Thoreau,..
Where's your nutcracker costume.
I'm the host Red Jay,...

A good host always establishes dominance with
his etiquette..
Besides guy,..
Onyx and I are performing The National...
(The puppet show about Julius Caesar
characterized as the Christ..)
"I thought you said you were having trouble with
the transfiguration."
Shhhhhhhh.
"Just tell me you rue."
....
"Caesar married Cleopatra in the Egyptian
manner didn't he Red Jay?"
(He shrugged)
Well I think we all know what that means...
Not really what,..
Ol Caesar consecrated himself??
"She may have helped him reach an empyrean
state of consciousness, yes Red Jay."
Said Obi sounding a little protective over the requiem.
....
Now that's pretty scary..
./...
""There he is!" said Obi as Onyx came into
the room

..
""**""""
!!!!! <Z>
Nice butler look Onyx. said Red Jay
Onyx was dressed like Obi, except his tuxedo
wasn't as wingy.

...
Obi looked like the fable count of Ginger Island.
Look at Red Jay Onyx,...
It's the most flexible guy in all Agora!(she)
Don't let any rebels go past without tearing your
oriented fly
Red Jay.(chi)
Real funny...
Aww you know I'm just kidding Red Jay,
"You look great."

The perfect combination of aggressive and proper.
Glorious demeanor!
Thanks Obi.
Just remember to take your hat off when the party settles down...
'You know I love that sleepover _vibe.'

....

''Well,..''
What are we waiting for,"
Are you boys ready to go to the party?
O yea.
''Don't forget your horns ...'' (she)
This is moose country!!!!

...

...

"Oh,"..
"I almost forgot my cape."

....

......

"The devils a horrible leader."
Muttered Red Jay wiping his mouth after just taking a swig.
'<>'"
'Hey,Which one of you scoundrels wore my cape in the forest!?"
THE END
"There's a spider web on my cape Red Jay!"

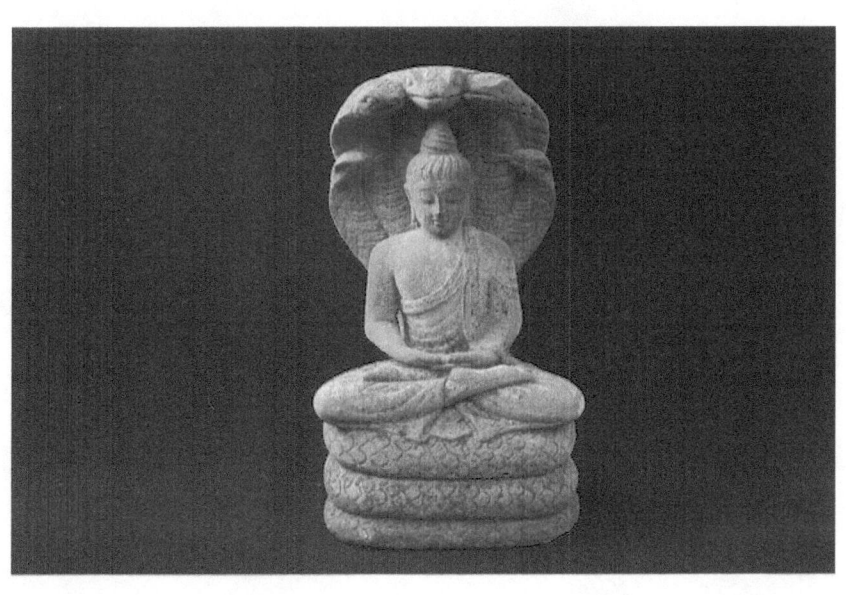

Z

www.ingramcontent.com/pod-product-compliance
Lightning Source LLC
Chambersburg PA
CBHW021038180526
45163CB00005B/2180